Letter and Number Tracing Book for Preschoolers: Learn How to Write Alphabet Upper and Lower Case and Numbers for Kids

ABCDEFGHIJKLMN
OPQRSTUVWXYZ
0123456789

Nina Noosita

Letter and Number Tracing Book for Preschoolers: Learn How to Write Alphabet Upper and Lower Case and Numbers for Kids

Copyright: Published in the United States by Nina Noosita
Published December 2018

ISBN: 9781790894840

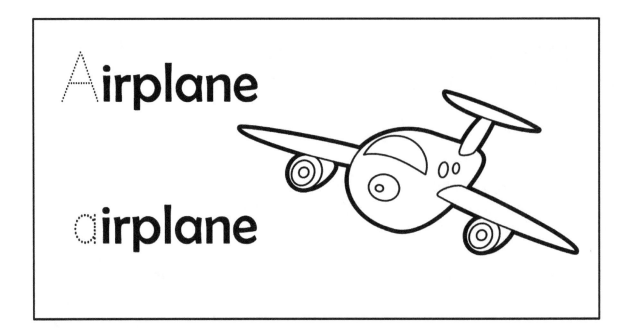

Airplane

airplane

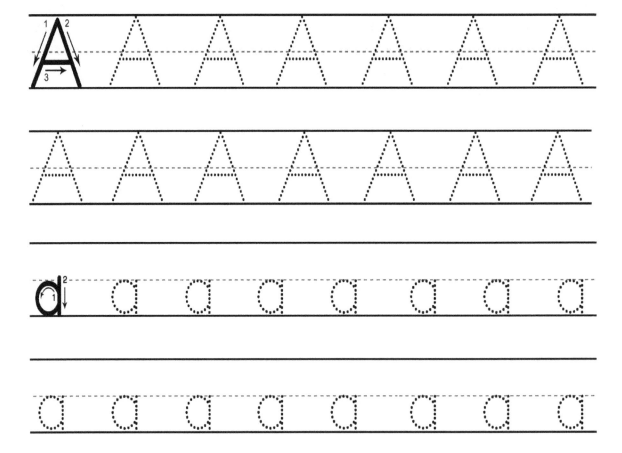

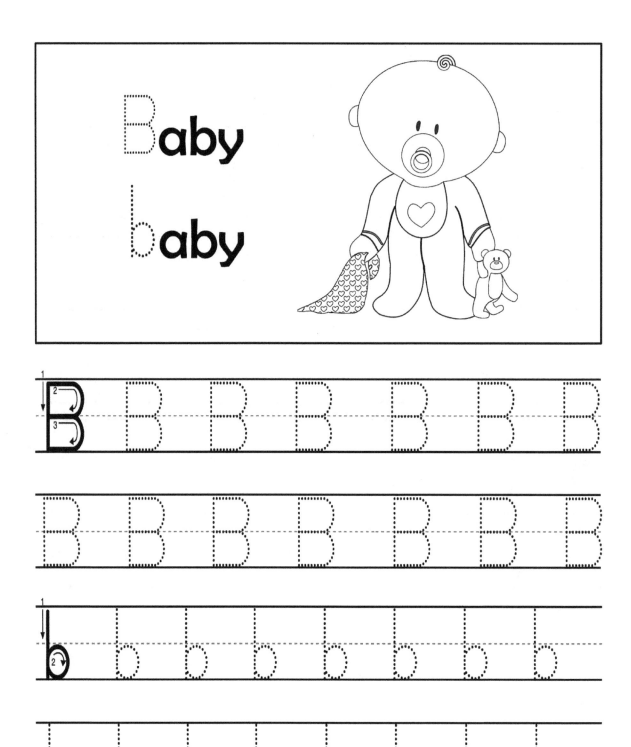

Baby

baby

B B B B B B B

B B B B B B B

B B B B B B B

B B B B B B B

b b b b b b b b

b b b b b b b b

b b b b b b b b

b b b b b b b b

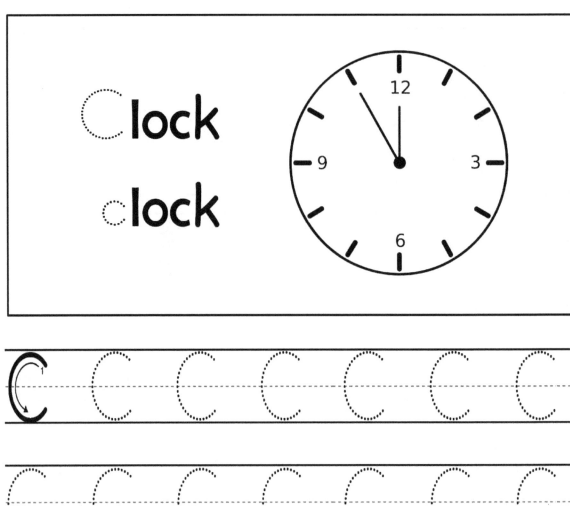

Clock

clock

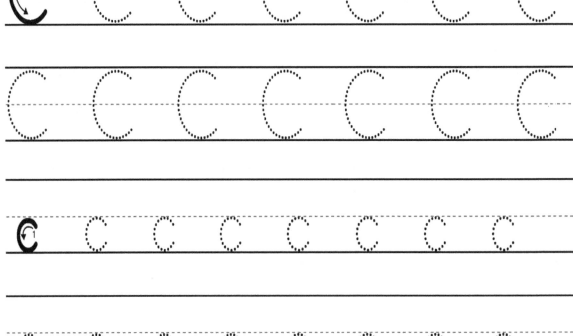

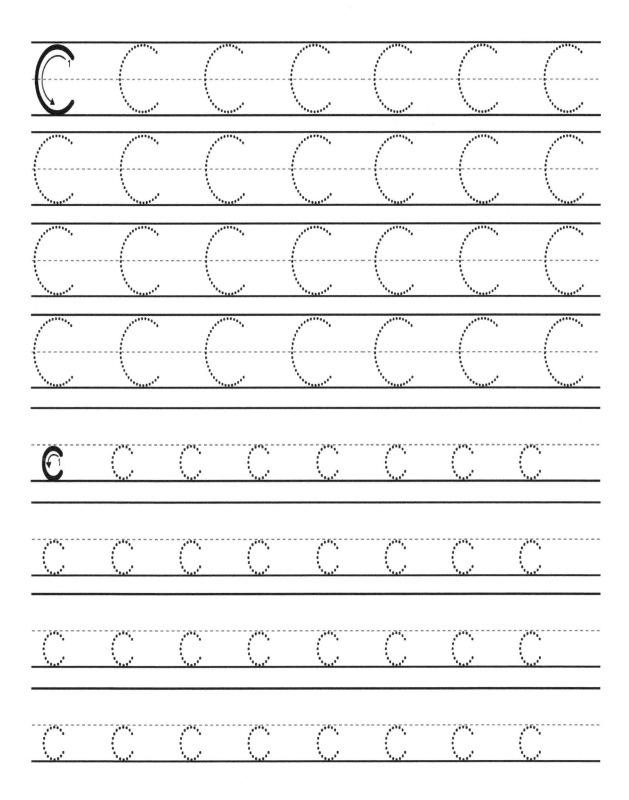

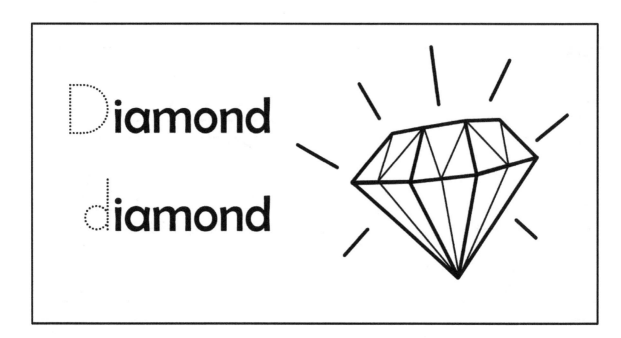

Diamond

diamond

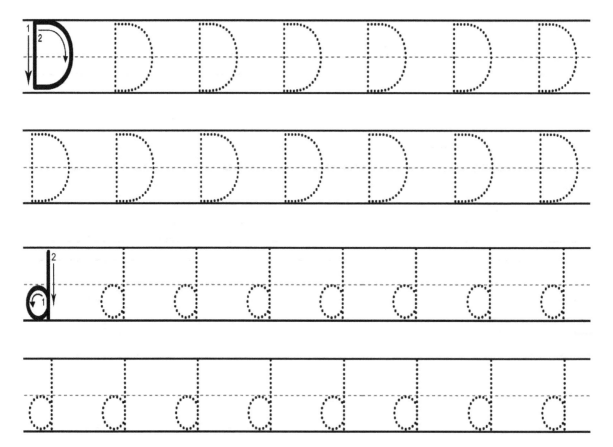

D D D D D D D

D D D D D D D

D D D D D D D

D D D D D D D

d d d d d d d d

d d d d d d d d

d d d d d d d d

d d d d d d d d

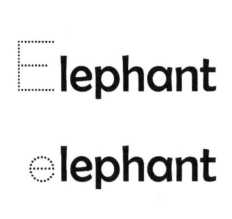 **lephant**

lephant

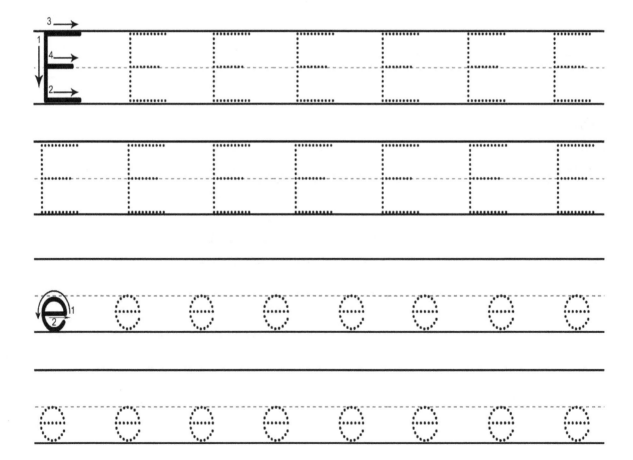

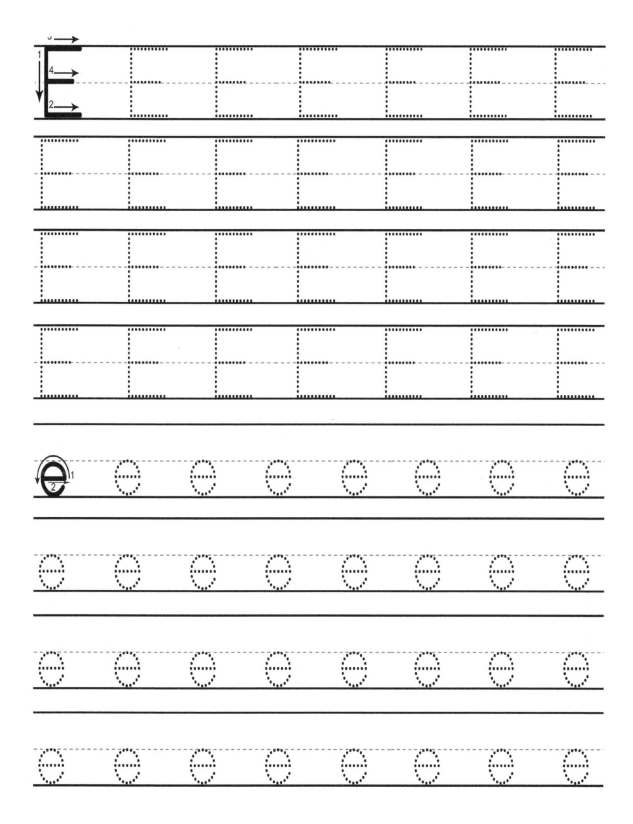

Fish

fish

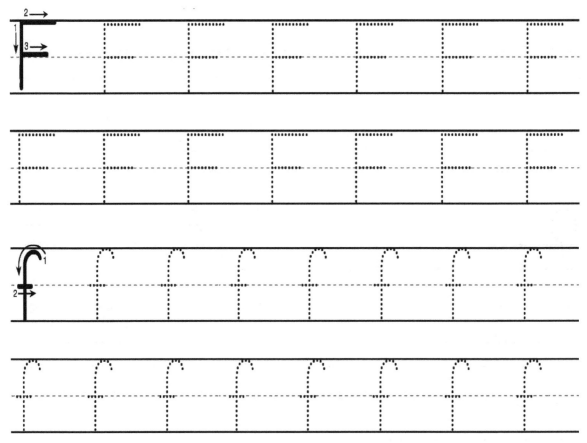

F F F F F F F

F F F F F F F

F F F F F F F

F F F F F F F

f f f f f f f f

f f f f f f f f

f f f f f f f f

f f f f f f f f

Giraffe

giraffe

G G G G G G G

G G G G G G G

g g g g g g g

g g g g g g g

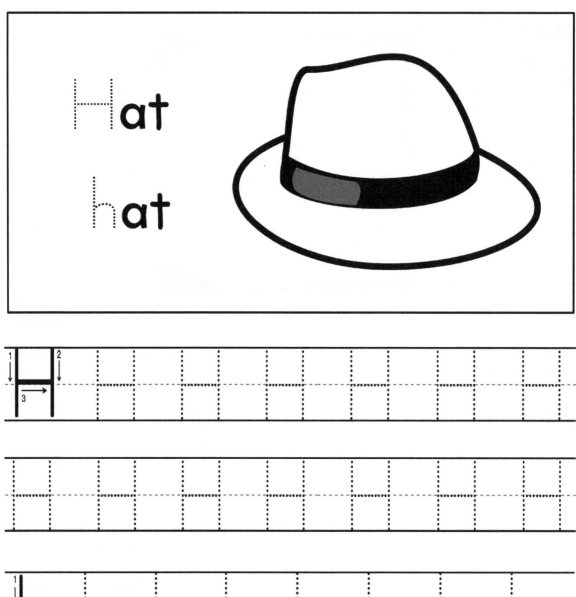

Hat

hat

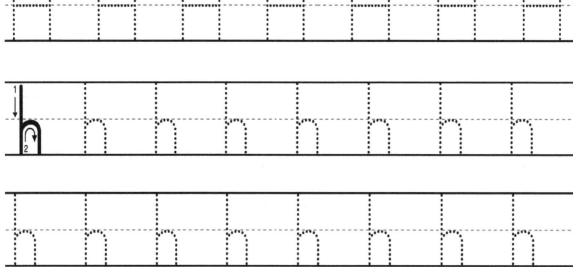

H h

(letter tracing practice worksheet for uppercase H and lowercase h)

Ice-cream

Ice-cream

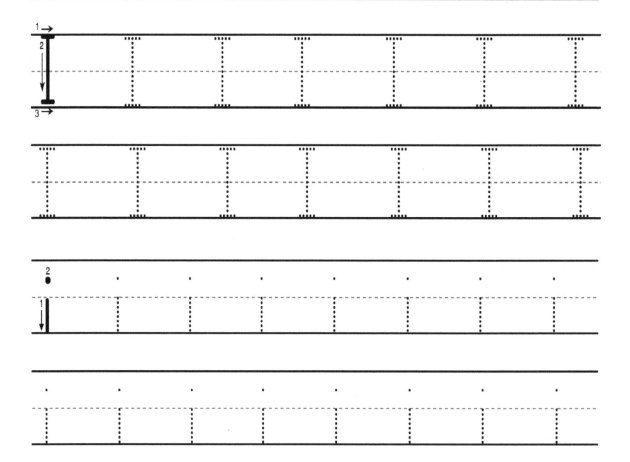

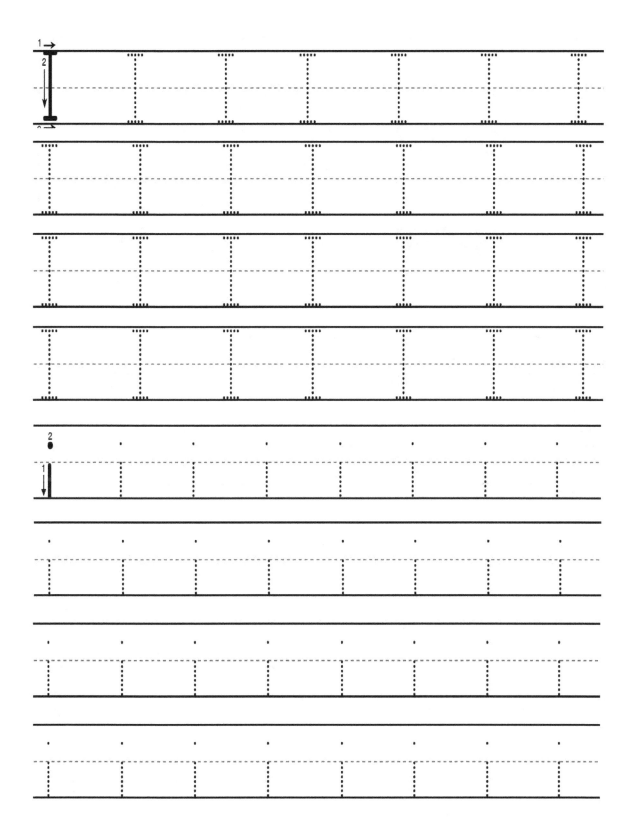

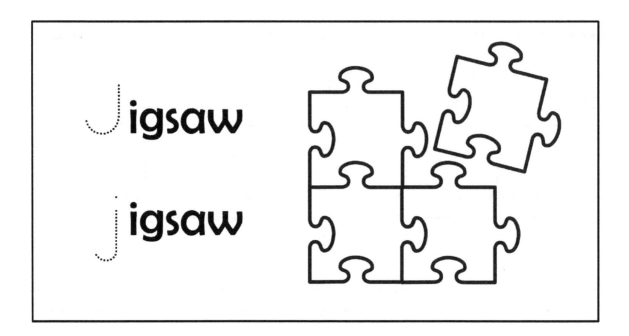

Jigsaw

Jigsaw

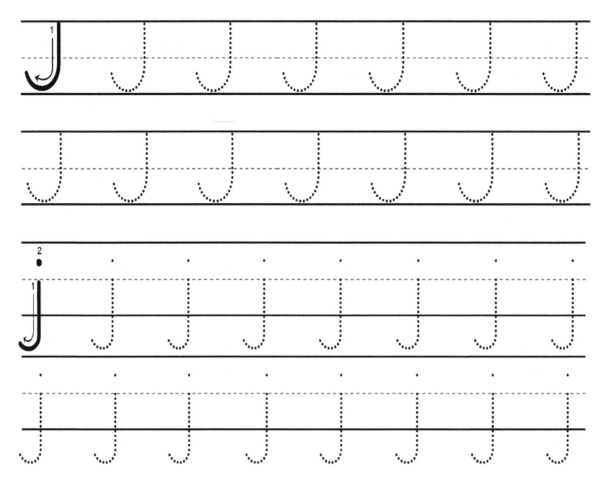

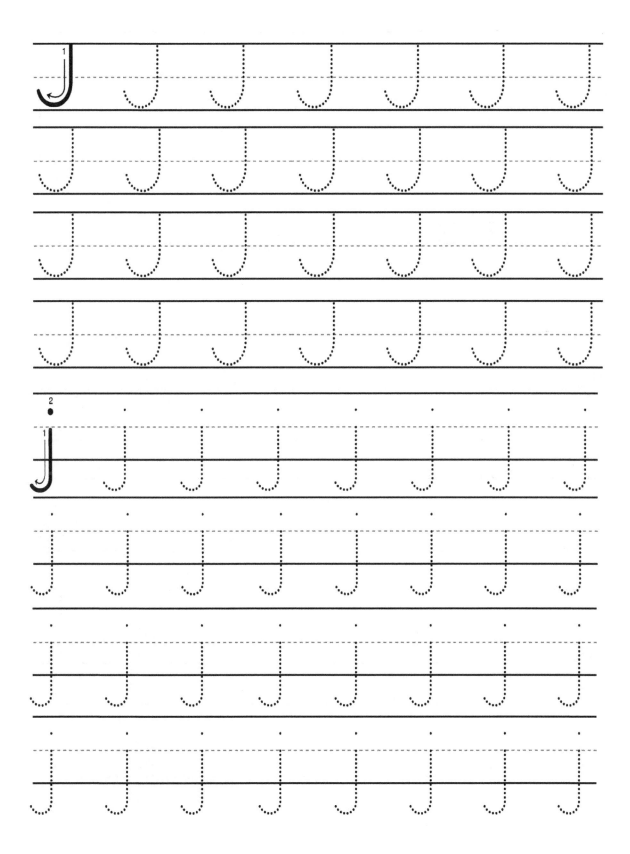

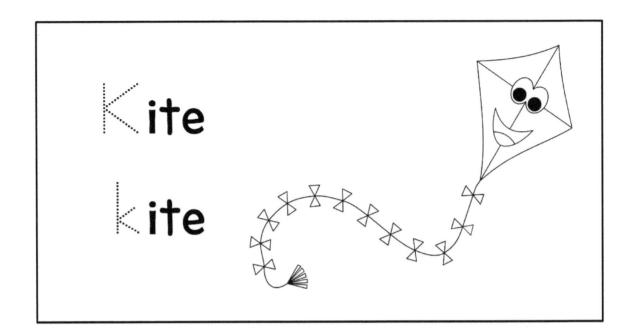

Kite

kite

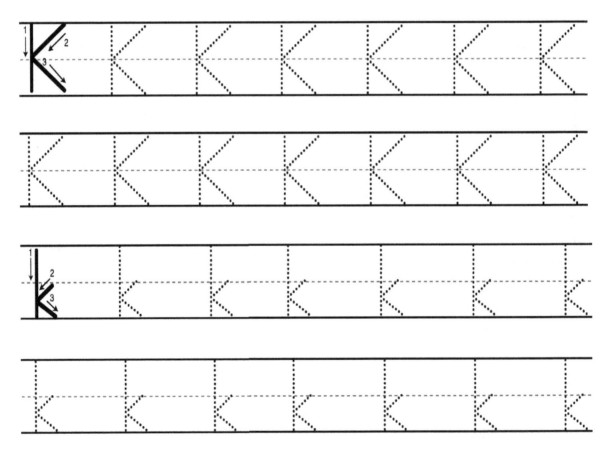

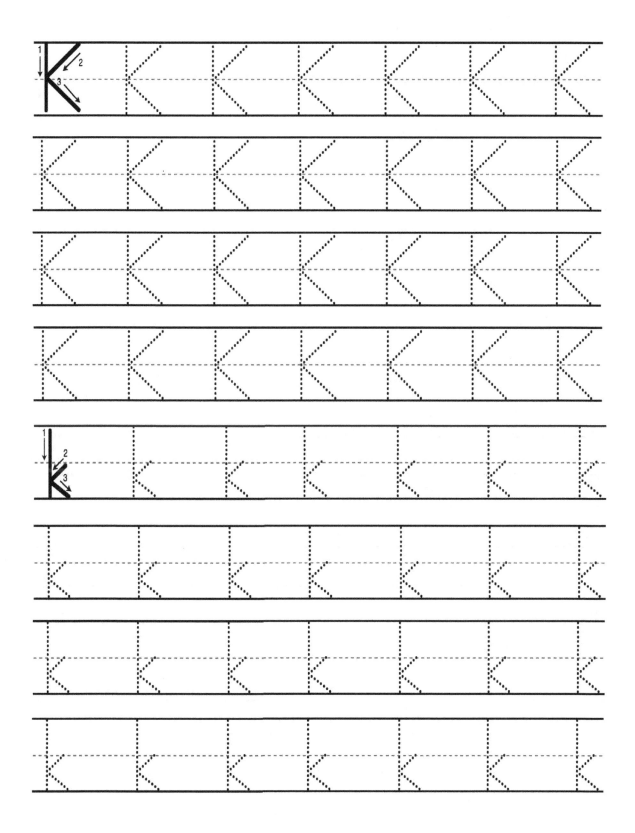

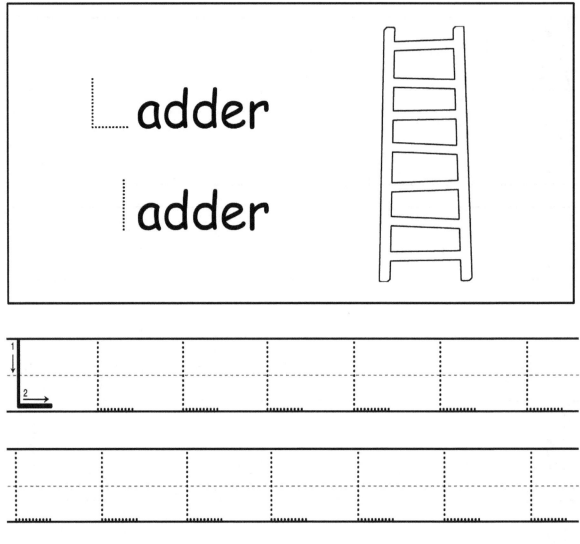

Ladder

ladder

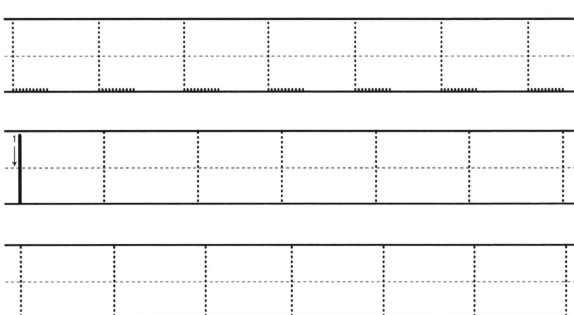

Monkey
monkey

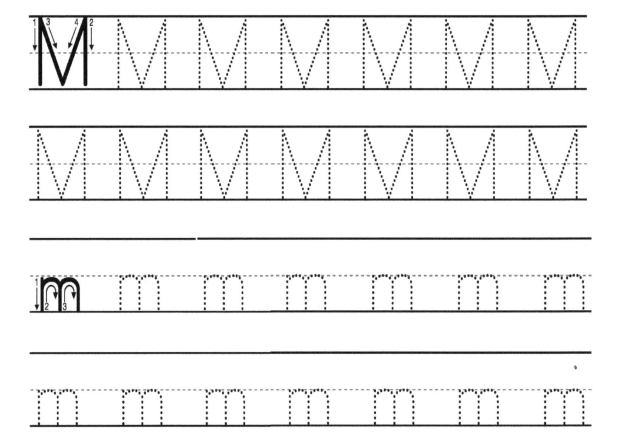

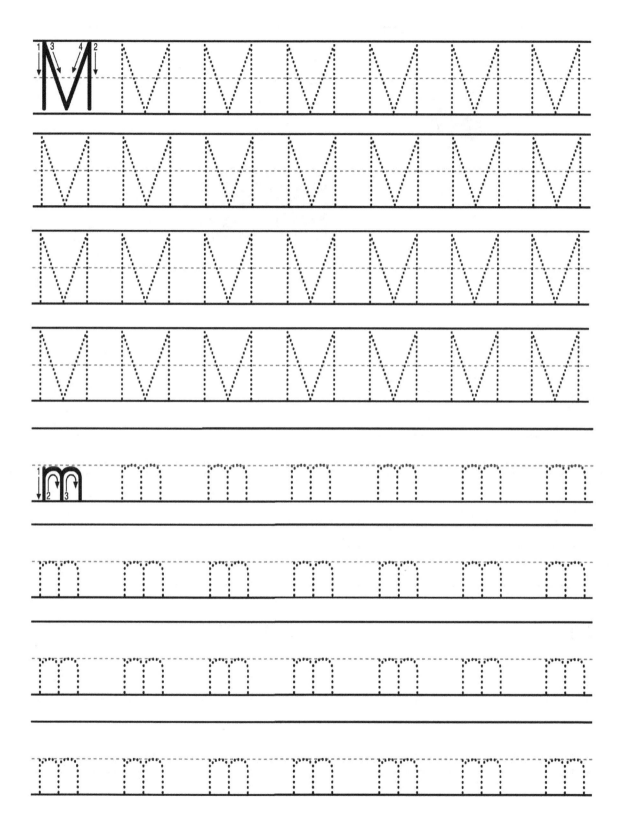

Nest

nest

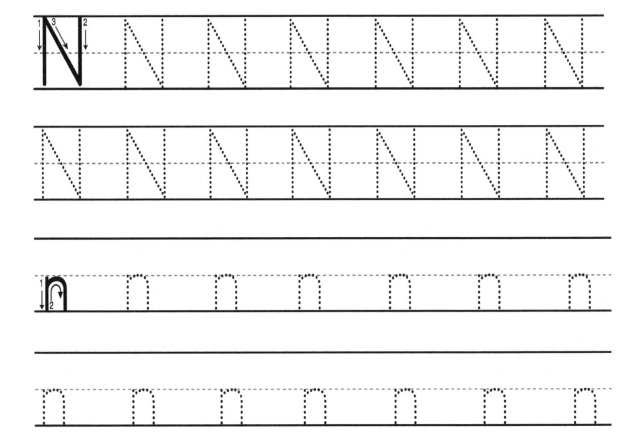

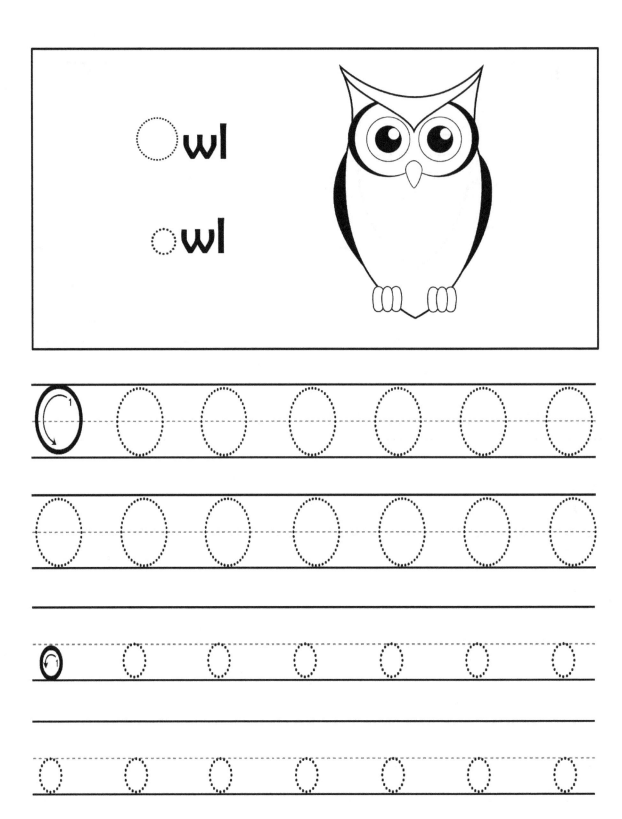

Owl

owl

Panda
panda

P P P P P P P P

P P P P P P P

p p p p p p p

p p p p p p p

P P P P P P P

P P P P P P P

P P P P P P P

P P P P P P P

p p p p p p p

p p p p p p p

p p p p p p p

p p p p p p p

Queen

queen

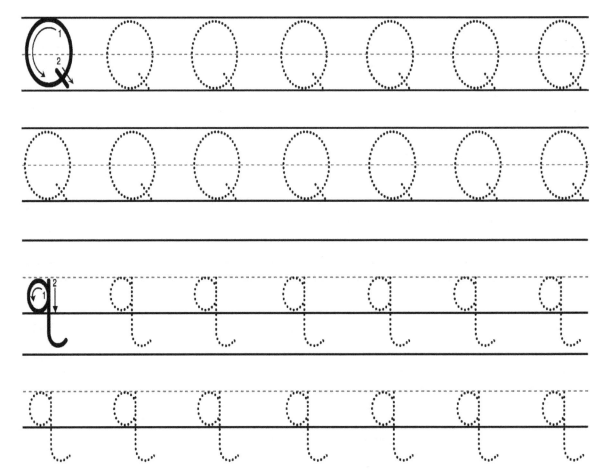

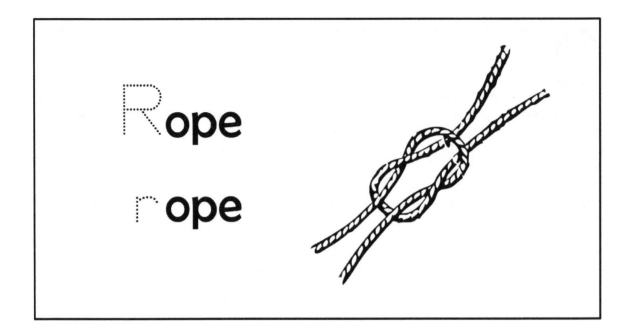

Rope

rope

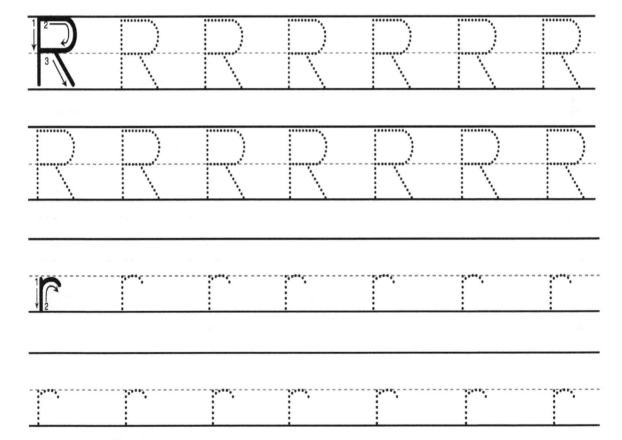

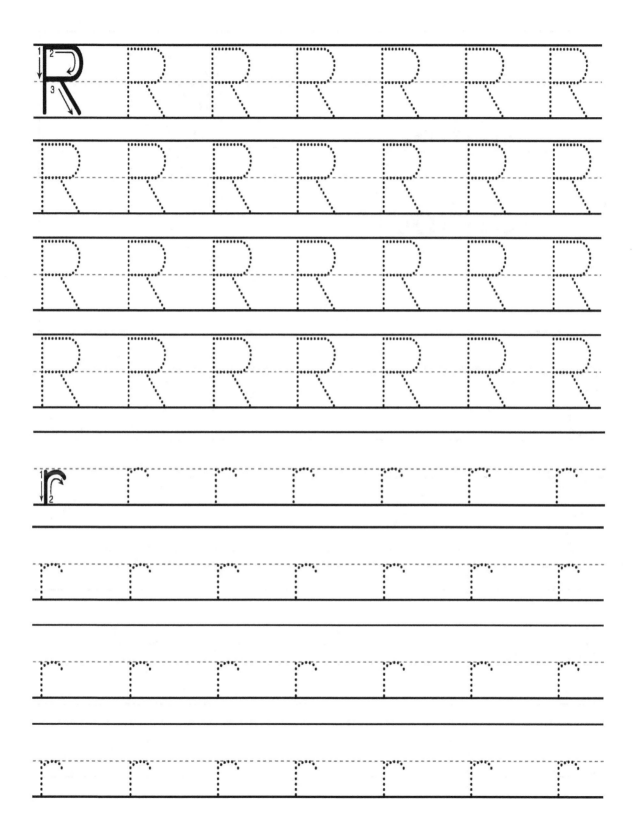

S unflower

s unflower

S S S S S S S S

S S S S S S S S

S s s s s s s s

s s s s s s s s

S S S S S S S

S S S S S S S

S S S S S S S

S S S S S S S

s s s s s s s

s s s s s s s

s s s s s s s

s s s s s s s

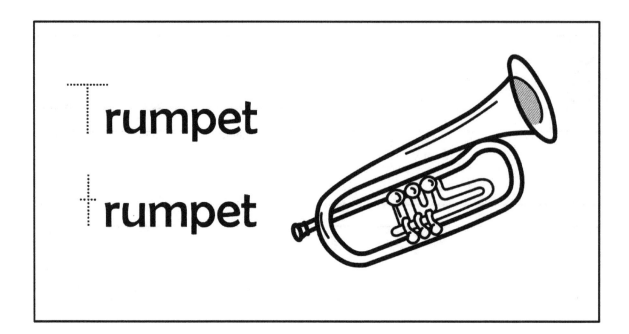

Trumpet

Trumpet

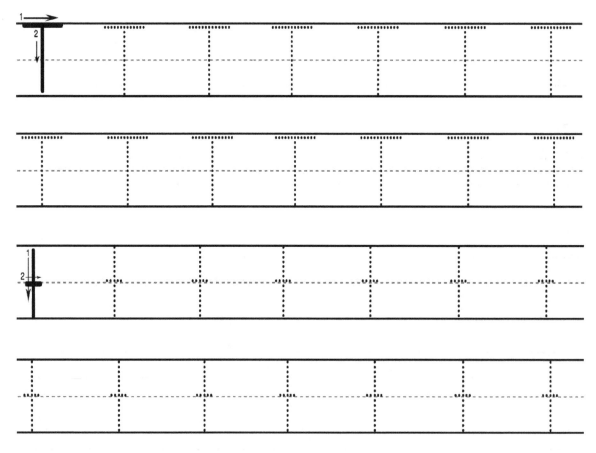

U nicorn

u nicorn

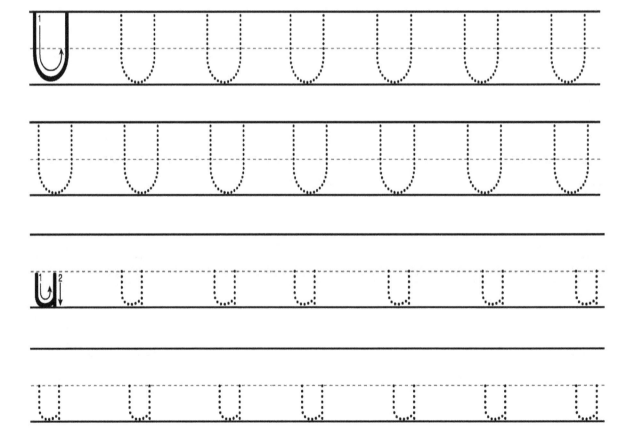

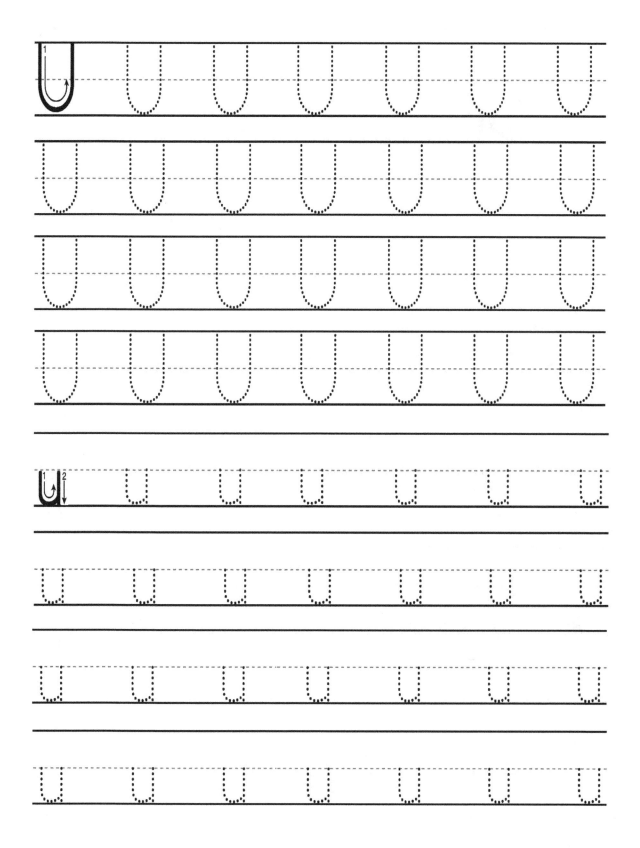

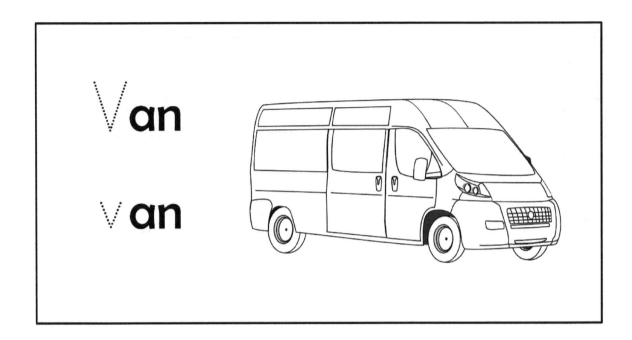

V an

v an

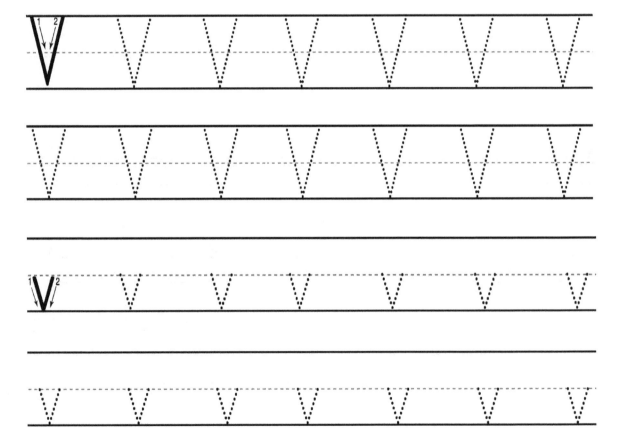

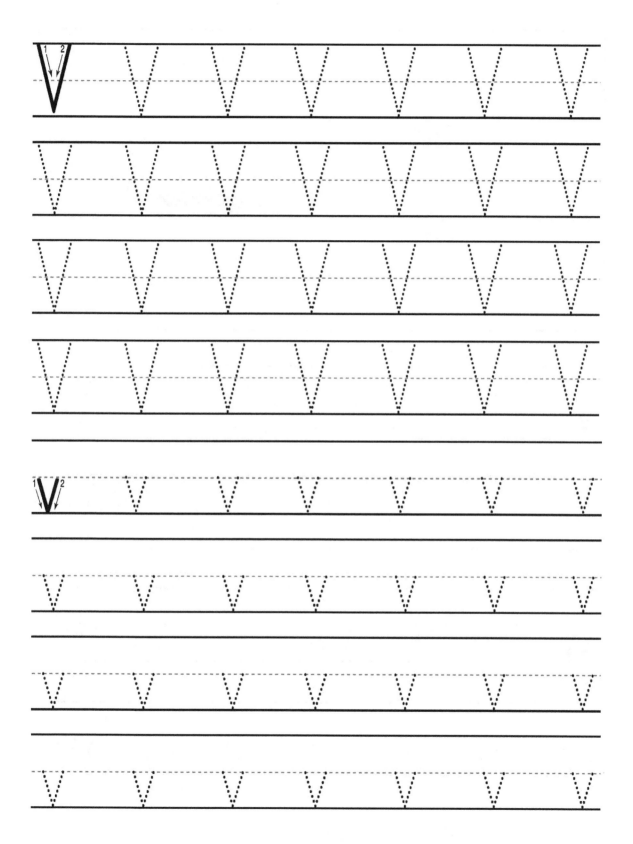

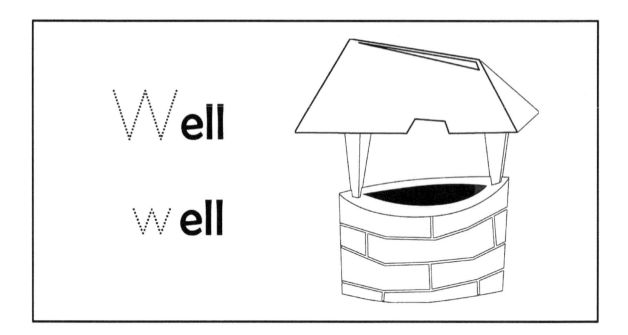

Well

well

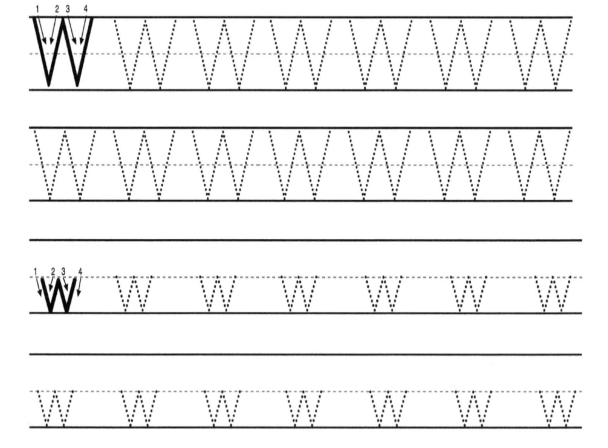

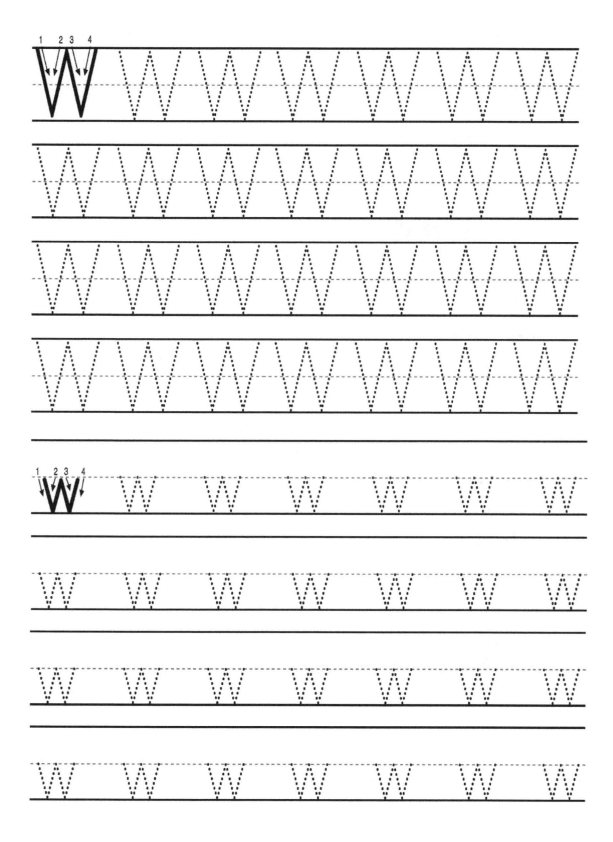

Xmas

xmas

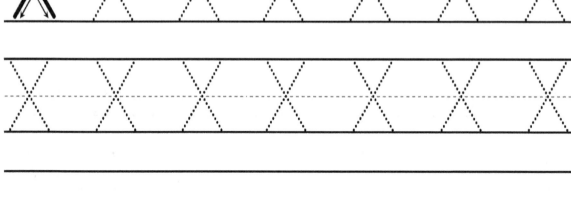

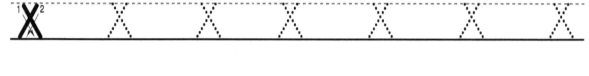

Y awn

y awn

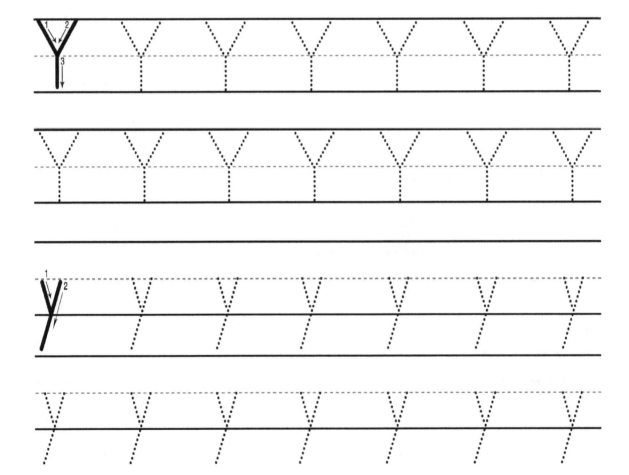

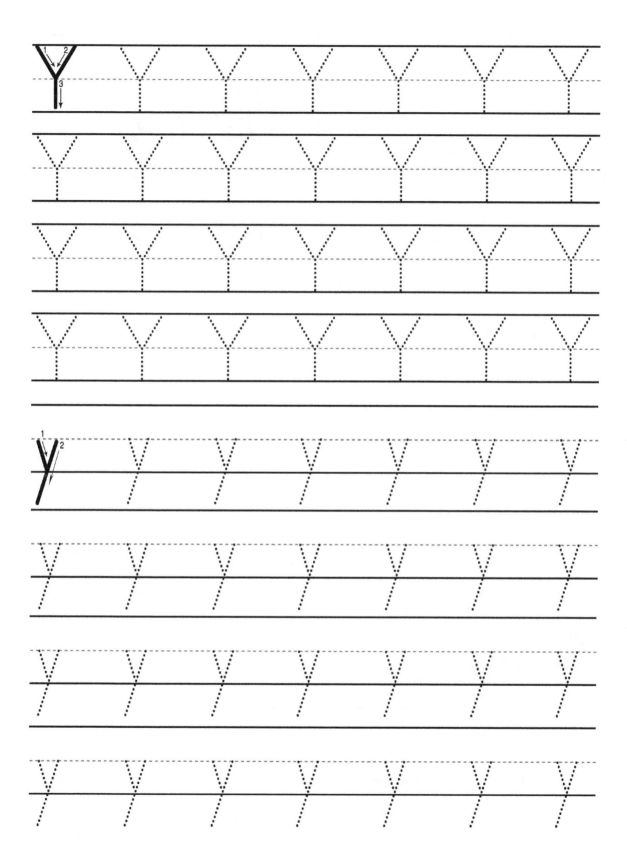

Zebra
zebra

1→ Z 2
Z
3→

1

How many ball?

Trace and write.

1 | 2
3 →

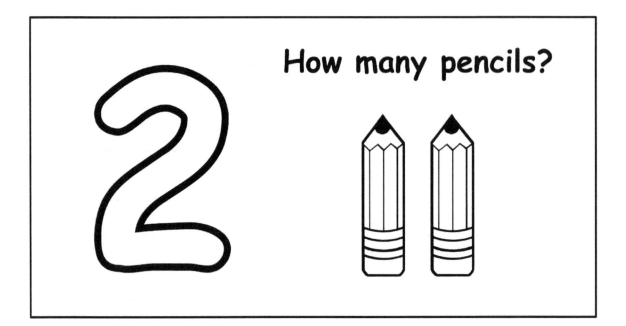

How many pencils?

Trace and write.

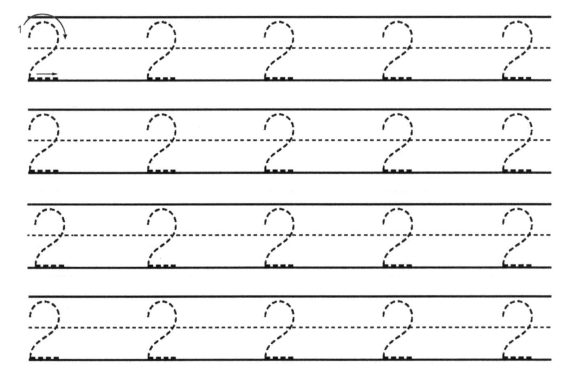

2 2 2 2 2

2 2 2 2 2

2 2 2 2 2

2 2 2 2 2

2 2 2 2 2

2 2 2 2 2

2 2 2 2 2

2 2 2 2 2

How many apples?

Trace and write.

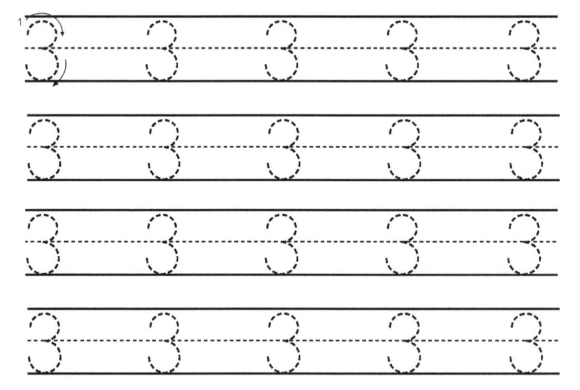

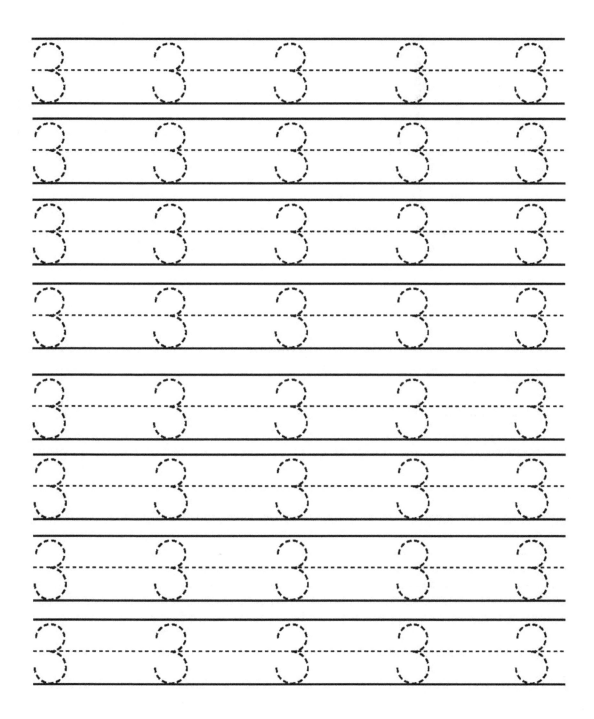

How many trees?

Trace and write.

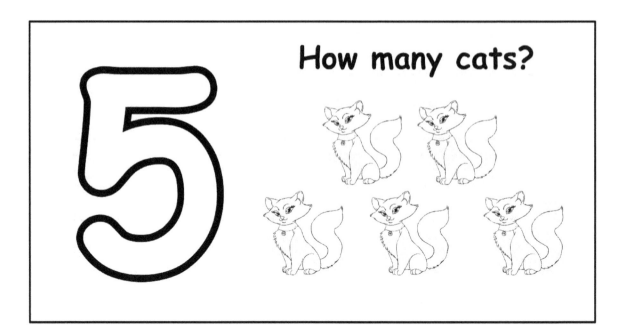

How many cats?

Trace and write.

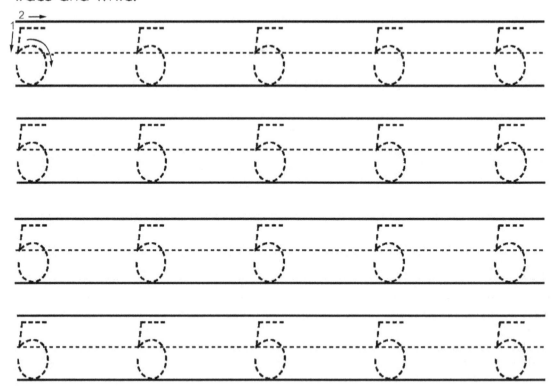

5 5 5 5 5

5 5 5 5 5

5 5 5 5 5

5 5 5 5 5

5 5 5 5 5

5 5 5 5 5

5 5 5 5 5

5 5 5 5 5

How many pigs?

Trace and write.

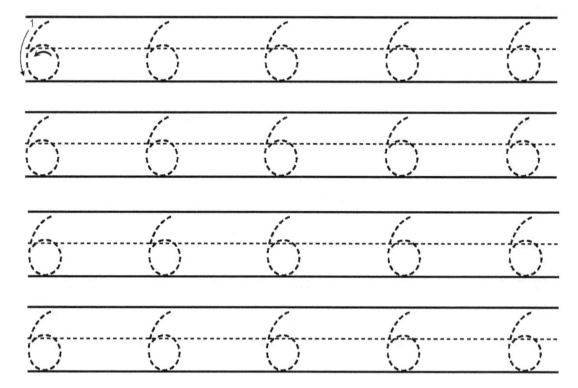

6 6 6 6 6

6 6 6 6 6

6 6 6 6 6

6 6 6 6 6

6 6 6 6 6

6 6 6 6 6

6 6 6 6 6

6 6 6 6 6

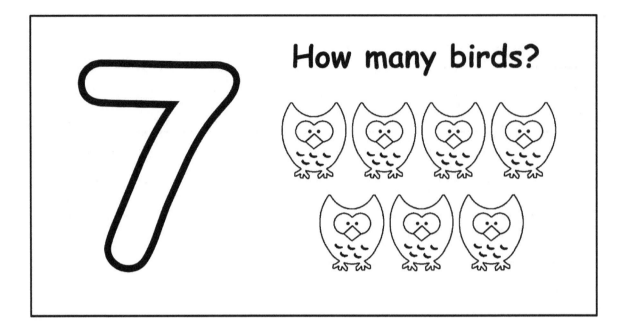

How many birds?

Trace and write.

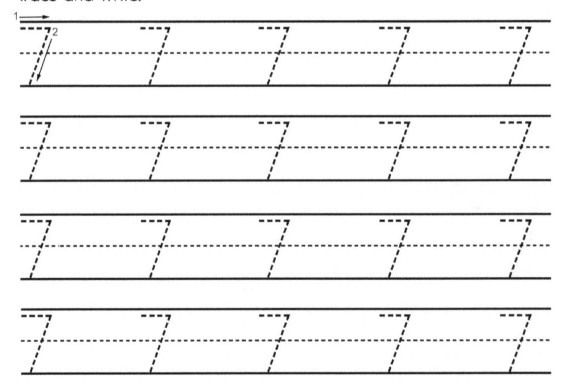

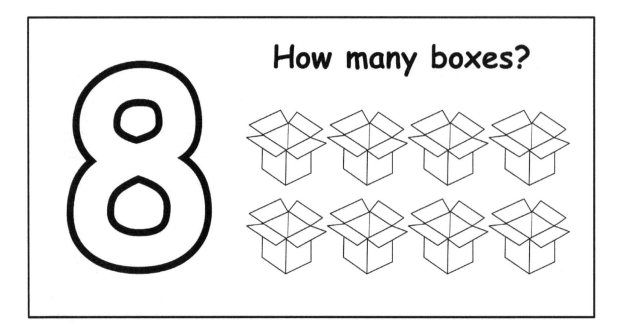

How many boxes?

Trace and write.

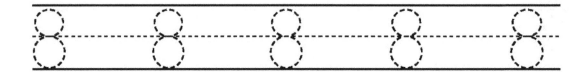

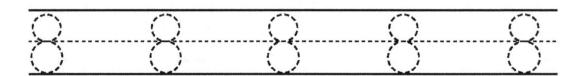

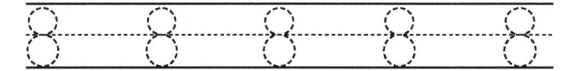

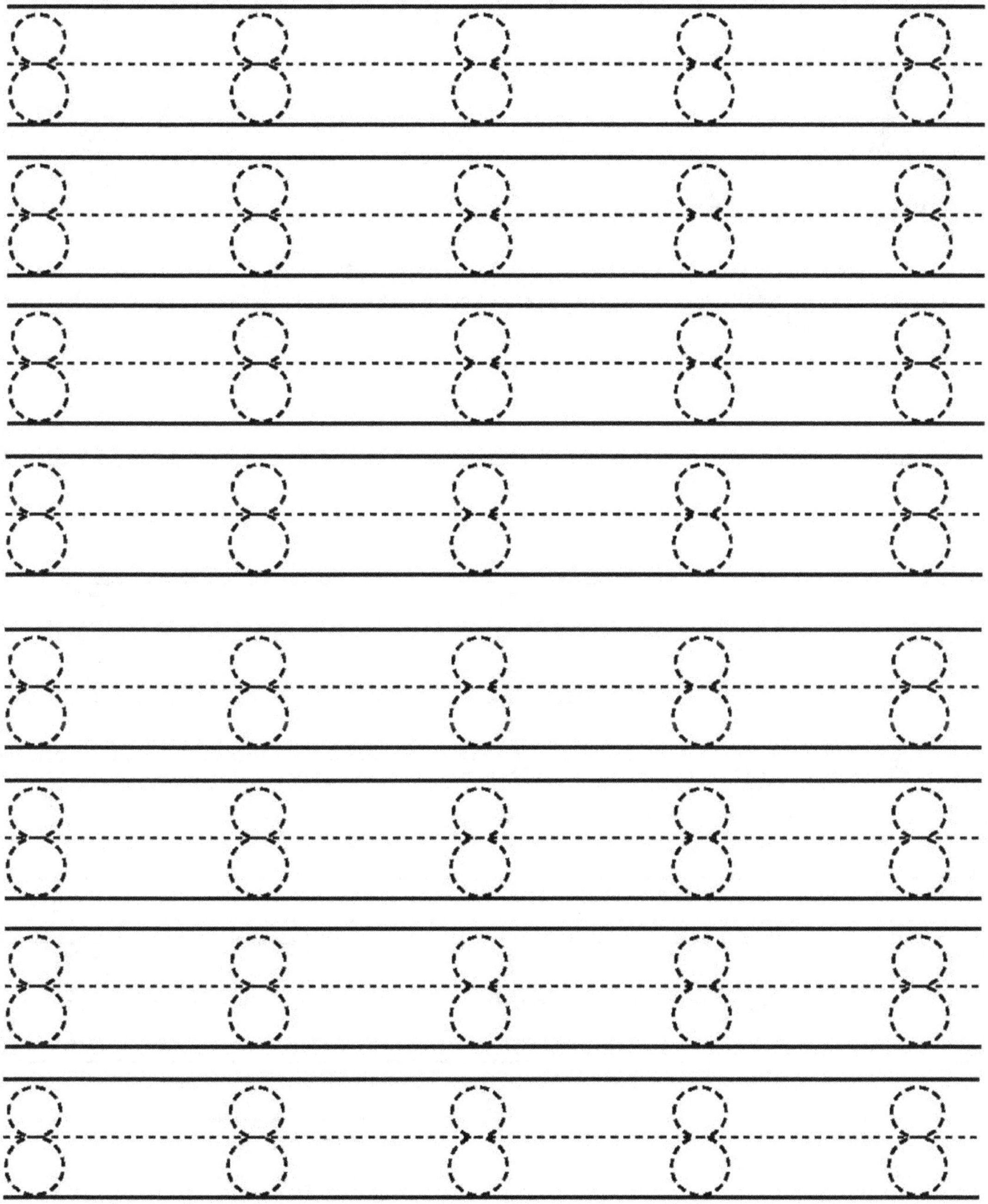

How many flowers?

Trace and write.

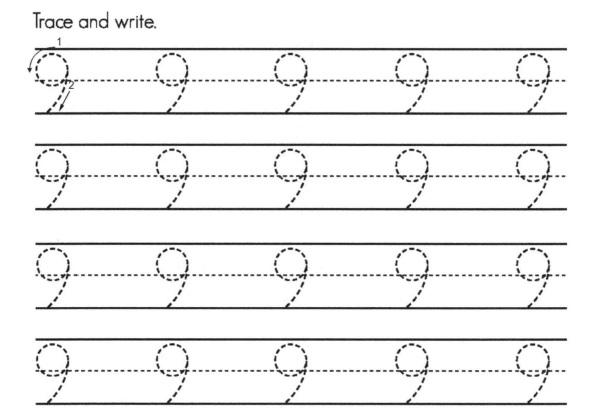

9 9 9 9 9

9 9 9 9 9

9 9 9 9 9

9 9 9 9 9

9 9 9 9 9

9 9 9 9 9

9 9 9 9 9

9 9 9 9 9

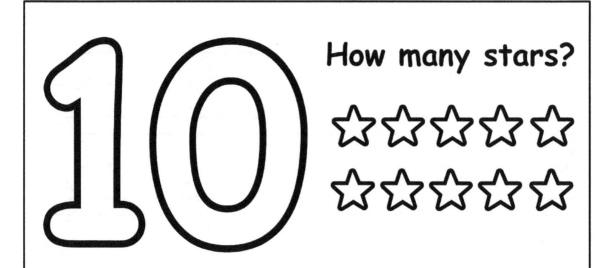

How many stars?

Trace and write.

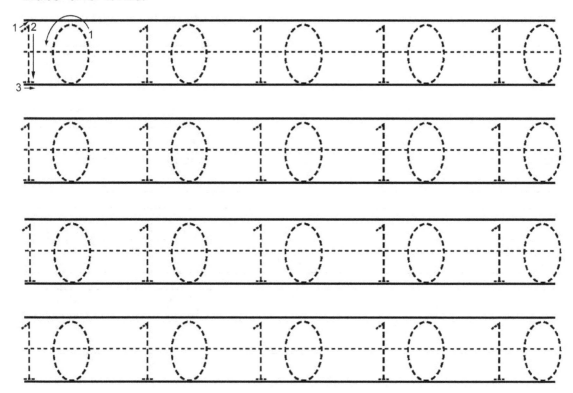

10 10 10 10 10

10 10 10 10 10

10 10 10 10 10

10 10 10 10 10

10 10 10 10 10

10 10 10 10 10

10 10 10 10 10

10 10 10 10 10

Thank you

CPSIA information can be obtained
at www.ICGtesting.com
Printed in the USA
LVHW061208160520
655721LV00008B/408

9 781790 894840